GREAT SPORTING EVENTS

Motorsports

Clive Gifford

W
FRANKLIN WATTS
LONDON · SYDNEY

First published in 2011 by Franklin Watts
338 Euston Road, London NW1 3BH

Franklin Watts Australia
Level 17/207 Kent Street, Sydney NSW 2000

Editors: Katie Dicker & Gerard Cheshire.
Art Direction: Cheena Yadav (Q2AMedia)
Designers: Kanika Kohli, Ravinder Kumar
(Q2AMedia)
Picture Researchers: Ankit Dubey, Sumedha
Chopra and Nivisha Sinha (Q2AMedia)

Picture credits:
t=top b=bottom c=centre l=left r=right

Front Cover: Jay LaPrete/AP Photo.
Back Cover: Ross Setford /NZPA/AP Photo,
Aijaz Rahi/AP Photo, Dave Thompson/AP Photo,
Mark J. Terrill/AP Photo, Jay LaPrete/AP Photo,
Anja Niedringhaus/AP Photo.
Title Page: David Vincent/AP Photo.
Imprint Page: Eckehard Schulz/AP Photo.
Insides: Eddie Worth/AP Photo: 4, Ong Chin
Kai/AP Photo: 5, Shuji Kajiyama/AP Photo: 6-7,
Mark Humphrey/AP Photo: 8, Mark Duncan/
AP Photo: 9, Rusty Kennedy/AP Photo: 10, Dale
Davis/AP Photo: 11, David Graham/AP Photo:
12, AP Photo: 13, David Vincent/AP Photo:
14-15, Wayne Drought/NZPA/AP Photo: 16,
Alastair Grant/AP Photo: 17, Natacha Pisarenko/
AP Photo: 18, Bernat Armangue/AP Photo: 19,
AP Photo: 20, Diego Azubel/AP Photo: 21, Gero
Breloer/AP Photo: 22, Paul Gilham/Getty Images
Sport/Getty Images: 23, Larry Lawrence/AMA
Pro Racing/AP Photo: 24, Luis M. Alvarez/AP
Photo: 25, Tom Hevezi/AP Photo: 26, Eckehard
Schulz/AP Photo: 27, Eddie Worth/AP Photo: 28.

Every attempt has been made to clear copyright.
Should there be any inadvertent omission, please
apply to the publisher for rectification.

A CIP catalogue record for this book
is available from the British Library.

ISBN: 978 1 4451 0192 7

Dewey Classification: 796.7

Note: At the time of going to press, the statistics in this
book were up to date. However, due to the nature of
sport, it is possible that some of these may now be out
of date.

Printed in China

Franklin Watts is a division of Hachette Children's
Books, an Hachette UK company.
www.hachette.co.uk

Contents

*Words in **bold** are in the glossary on page 30

High-speed races

Motor vehicles were invented and developed in the late nineteenth century. It wasn't long before they were raced against each other in exciting competitions. Today, motorsports fans flock to events in thousands to see racing at incredibly high speeds.

Fast action

The first ever motor race was from Paris to Rouen in France in 1894. It was completed at an average speed of 16.54km/h (10.27mph). Today's racing cars and motorcycles frequently race at speeds of over 300km/h (186.4mph).

On track

Motorsports events take place off-road or on track **circuits**. Many tracks are oval-shaped, with long straights and large 180° bends. Others, such as the Pocono Raceway in Pennsylvania, USA, are tri-ovals with three bends of 120° and three straights. Formula 1 cars (see pages 20–23) and some motorbikes also race on street circuits, which have lots of dramatic twists and turns.

Formula 1 cars **accelerate** at the start of a 1967 race at the famous Brands Hatch circuit in England.

All types

Whilst leading NASCAR (see pages 10–11) and Formula 1 (see pages 20–21) drivers are paid large sums of money to race, thousands of motorsports enthusiasts are **amateurs** who race for the thrill and the challenge. Almost all types of vehicle are raced in some sort of competition; from ride-on lawn mowers and school buses to the cabs of articulated trucks.

Start in karts

Karting is scaled-down racing in cars that sit very low to the ground. These are usually raced around small circuits with races lasting around 15 minutes. Many leading racing drivers, including Britain's Lewis Hamilton and Germany's Michael Schumacher, began their careers in karting. At the highest level, Division 1 Superkarts are fearsome racing machines with top speeds of just over 250km/h (155mph).

Karts compete in the Singapore National Championships race. The karts complete each lap of the course at an average speed of 80km/h (50mph).

GREAT SPORTING STATS

The fastest race vehicles of all are top fuel dragsters, which race in pairs along a straight track called a drag strip. In 2009, US dragster driver Larry Dixon reached a speed of 517.53km/h (321mph). His race on the 305-metre long drag strip lasted less than 3.9 seconds!

The IndyCar Series

Open-wheel racing features single-seater cars with drivers in open **cockpits**. They race around circuits made of smooth track. In North America, the most popular form of open-wheel racing is the IndyCar Series.

Long history, new start

For 30 years, there were two different competitions for US open-wheel racing, Indy Racing and CART or CHAMP cars. In 2008, these merged to form one competition, the IndyCar Series, run by the Indy Racing League. This organisation also runs the Indy Lights competition (with over 13 races in 2010) for younger drivers.

Identical vehicles

Each IndyCar race team uses very similar cars, which helps to make the races close and exciting. Each team's cars use Honda engines that produce around four times as much power as a family saloon car engine. These engines run on **ethanol** which is less likely to accidentally catch light and causes less pollution than any other fuel.

New Zealander Scott Dixon races his IndyCar around the Twin Ring Motegi circuit in Japan. His race vehicle can reach speeds of over 320km/h (199mph) on fast tracks.

Racing season

The IndyCar season begins in March and runs until October. It comprises 17 races. Races mostly take place in the USA, but are also held in Canada, Brazil and Japan. They are mainly held in the afternoon on oval tracks, such as the Indianapolis Motor Speedway (see page 8), but the race calendar also includes some night races and some street circuit competitions, such as the Honda Indy Toronto in Canada and the Sao Paulo 300 in Brazil. For each race, teams adjust the **suspension** and **handling** of the cars to suit the circuit.

Points scoring

The race winner receives 50 points, second place 40 points and the points descend to 10 for each team sitting between 25th and 33rd in the race. In addition, the driver who leads the most laps receives two points and the **pole sitter** gets 1 point. In 2006, US driver Sam Hornish Jr. and Britain's Dan Wheldon were both leading with 475 points, but the IndyCar championship prize went to Hornish because he had won more races.

GREAT SPORTING STATS

IndyCars usually race at top speeds of around 370km/h (230mph). The fastest recorded speed was in 1996 when Canada's Paul Tracy drove his car at 413.52km/h (256.9mph) at the Michigan International Speedway, USA.

Danica Patrick, one of the most successful female racing drivers, shows off her trophy after winning the Indy Japan 300 in 2008.

Indianapolis 500

The Indy 500 is IndyCar's most famous race and one of the most prestigious races in the world. Held since 1911 at the Indianapolis Motor Speedway in the USA, an estimated audience of 400,000 race fans attend the race weekend at the end of May.

The Brickyard

Built in 1908, the 4.02km (2.5 miles) oval track was originally made from crushed rock and tar, which proved dangerous as ruts and holes formed and loose stones would fly up and hit drivers. It was then covered in 3.2 million bricks in sand to provide a new racing surface, earning it the nickname 'The Brickyard'. The bricks are now covered in a layer of **asphalt**, but nine rows remain exposed at the finish line. Winners of the Indy 500 often kiss the bricks after getting out of their cars.

Pole sitter Helio Castroneves leads at the 2009 Indy 500, so named as it covers 500 miles (805km).

Qualifying and bumping

Practice and **qualifying** for the race begins several weeks before the actual race day. Drivers perform timed trials over four laps of the track with the fastest made the pole sitter – the car in the best starting position for the final race. A total of 33 cars compete in the final. The driver placed 33rd has a difficult time because any other qualifier who records a faster time in the timed trials will take his place in the final. This is known as bumping.

Race champions

Three American racing greats, Rick Mears, A.J. Foyt and Al Unser, have all won the Indy 500 four times. Unser is part of a great racing family. His brother Bobby won three Indy 500s and his son, Al Unser Jr, has won the race twice. In recent years, champions have come from as far afield as Britain, Brazil and New Zealand.

GREAT SPORTING STATS

During the 1996 Indy 500, Eddie Cheever completed a lap at 379.9km/h (236mph) – the fastest race lap ever. Sarah Fisher completed a 2002 qualifying lap of the Indy 500 at an average speed of 369km/h (229mph) – the fastest by a female driver.

Rick Mears wins his fourth Indy 500 in 1991. The Borg-Warner Trophy features the sculptured faces of more than 90 winners of the race. Winners traditionally celebrate by drinking a bottle of milk.

NASCAR

The National Association for **Stock Car** Auto Racing (NASCAR) is the leading stock car association in the world. It was formed by race driver and promoter Bill France Senior in 1948. Since that time, it has become the USA's most popular form of car racing.

The Sprint Cup

NASCAR runs a large range of competitions, including races for pick-up trucks and up-and-coming drivers. Its leading competition, however, is the Sprint Cup. This competition is watched by millions of people over its 36 races. It begins in February and ends in November.

The cars

The cars used in Sprint Cup racing are stripped-down vehicles with steel panelled bodies, few electronic aids and no wing mirrors. They have sturdy roll-cages to protect the drivers and enormously powerful engines, which can take cars to speeds of over 310km/h (192.6 miles).

US driver Greg Sacks' NASCAR vehicle goes flying through the air after a high speed crash during the AC Spark Plug 500 NASCAR race.

Close racing

Qualifying takes place on the Friday before the race. It is based on the drivers' fastest times over two laps and determines the order in which drivers take up their starting positions. A maximum **field** of 43 cars is allowed in a Sprint Cup race. This can lead to incredibly tight racing, with frequent shunts and some crashes during the three to four hours it takes to complete an 805km (500 mile) race.

Chase for the championship

In 2004 a change to the racing points system was introduced. After the first 26 races, the top 12 drivers now have their points raised to 5,000, plus 10 points per race win. These 12 drivers compete in the regular field for the next ten races, but with their extra points they are the only drivers able to win the championship. The USA's Jimmie Johnson has recently dominated with four victories (2006–09).

Jimmie Johnson, in car No 48, leads during the Aaron's 499 NASCAR race at the Talladega Superspeedway in 2010.

GREAT SPORTING STATS

One closely-watched NASCAR statistic is the number of changes of race leader in a race. In the 2010 Sprint Cup, there was an average of 25.4 lead changes per race — the highest ever. In total 55 different drivers led a race for at least one lap.

Daytona 500

NASCAR's Sprint Cup includes the Daytona 500, a 500 mile-long race over 200 laps of the Daytona International Speedway, in Florida, USA. The winner receives over US$1.5 million (£1 million) and a replica of the famous Harley J. Earl Trophy.

A crowd of many thousands at the Daytona International Speedway track watch the Daytona 500.

Daytona International Speedway

The Daytona International Speedway is the venue for Superbike motorcycle racing, and a 24-hour **endurance** race, as well as the Daytona 500. Inside the tri-oval track is a lake, Lake Lloyd, and seating for over 160,000 race fans.

Start of the season

The Daytona 500 is held in the middle of February and is the very first points-scoring race of the NASCAR season. Qualifying occurs the weekend before to determine the order of the 43 cars in the big race.

An open race

Qualifying in pole position is no guarantee of success – only nine pole sitters have won in 51 races. Exciting overtaking, crashes and changes of lead are commonplace. In 2009, for example, Matt Kenseth started the race in 43rd place and went on to win.

Close finishes

The first Daytona 500, in 1959, ended in a **photo finish** as two cars crossed the line at almost the same time. The winner was Lee Petty, the father of NASCAR legend Richard Petty (see panel). Other close finishes include the 2007 race where Kevin Harvick beat Mark Martin by a tiny margin of just 0.02 seconds.

GREAT SPORTING STATS

The great Richard Petty (Nascar career: 1958–1992) is one of NASCAR's all-time leading drivers. 'The King', as he was nicknamed, won 200 NASCAR races including a record seven Daytona 500 victories. Only eight times has the winner of the Daytona 500 gone on to win the entire NASCAR championship. Richard Petty achieved this feat four times.

Richard Petty speeds round the Daytona track during practice for the 1968 Daytona 500. Petty won Daytona 500 races in the 1960s, 1970s and 1980s.

Le Mans 24 Hours

Endurance races last many hours. The most famous of all is the Le Mans 24 Hour race in France. Teams of three relaying drivers, with one car, race for an entire 24 hours non-stop. The winning team is the one that covers the greatest distance in that time.

During the Le Mans 24 Hour race, drivers use headlamps to race through the night.

Circuit de la Sarthe

The Le Mans race was first held on the historic Circuit de la Sarthe, back in 1923. Over the years, it has undergone many changes and is now 13.65km (8.48 miles) long. One of its most famous features is the Mulsanne Straight where speeds can exceed 300km/h (186mph), before heavy braking gets cars down to 50–70km/h (31–43mph) so that they can travel through the tight Mulsanne Corner without leaving the track.

Race start

Around 50 cars take part in Le Mans, which is held in June each year. In 2010, the race was watched by 238,850 spectators. Up until 1970, the drivers ran from one side of the track and jumped into their cars to start the race. Now, drivers begin with a **rolling start** in the afternoon and race through the night and into the next day.

14

Teams and stops

In 1982, Belgium's Jackie Ickx and Britain's Derek Bell became the last two-driver team to win Le Mans. All cars now have three drivers, none of whom can drive for more than four hours at a time. Swapping drivers, refuelling, fitting new tyres and running repairs mean that cars make a number of **pit stops** throughout the race.

Le Mans legends

Some drivers love Le Mans. Henri Pescarolo from France has raced there a record 33 times, winning four times. Denmark's Tom Kristensen holds the record for most wins with eight; in 1997, 2008 and a run of six in a row 2000–2005. Seven of his eight wins came in Audi cars. The other win was in a Bentley Speed 8. Porsche remains the leading make of car with 16 Le Mans wins.

Tom Kristensen raises his hand in celebration as he crosses the finish line to win the Le Mans race in 2008.

GREAT SPORTING STATS

The 2010 Le Mans winners — Germany's Mike Rockenfeller and Timo Bernhard and France's Romain Dumas completed 397 laps of the track as they covered a distance of around 5,410km (3361.6 miles). This works out at an average speed of over 225km/h (140mph).

World Rally Championship

In rally races, cars race on-road and off-road over a series of timed stages. The peak of rallying is the World Rally Championship (WRC). Hugely popular, crowds of over half a million people can gather to watch the various stages of a WRC rally.

Rally calendar

The WRC competition began in 1973. Over the years, the number of rallies held each season has changed. In 2010, the competition featured 13 races from February to November.

In between, teams travel the world to compete in rallies in countries such as Jordan, Japan, Mexico and New Zealand. The remaining rallies are all held in Europe.

Norway's Henning Solberg takes to the air as he negotiates a narrow bridge during Rally New Zealand.

Rally stages

Each rally lasts three days and is divided into 14–35 stages, with a typical day's racing covering 400km (248.5 miles). The various stages of each race may be on different surfaces, from loose sand and gravel to icy and snow. These offer different challenges to the skills and reactions of the driver and **co-driver** or navigator.

Championship points

Cars race against the clock, trying to record quicker times than their rivals. The winner of a rally scores ten points, with second place awarded eight points. The following six cars score points from six down to one. These points count towards the drivers' championship. A driver may race alone or as part of a team. Points won by a team's top two cars count towards the manufacturers' championship.

GREAT SPORTING STATS

Sébastien Loeb has an incredible World Rally Championship record. The French driver has won 54 WRC rallies and finished in the top three 29 more times. These victories have propelled Loeb to a record seven championships in a row (2004–2010).

Sébastien Loeb (right), of France, and co-driver Daniel Elena, of Monte Carlo, celebrate with the WRC drivers championship trophy.

The Dakar Rally

First held in 1978, the Dakar Rally is the ultimate long-distance motorsports event. Every year, cars, motorbikes, quadbikes and trucks race for over two weeks across more than 9,000km (5,600 miles) of challenging, tough terrain.

France's David Fretigne competes during the Dakar Rally, 2010.

The rally route

Traditionally, the race began in Paris and ended in the Senegal city of Dakar. In 1977, French motorcycle racer, Thierry Sabine, got lost in the African desert during the Abidjan-Nice rally. He decided to create an epic long-distance race from his home country, France, through the desert.

However, this route has been altered a number of times. For example, in 1995 it began in the Spanish city of Grenada, and in 2009, after security worries in Africa, the entire rally was moved to South America where it ran through Argentina and Chile.

Racing classes

Every year there are several winners of the Dakar Rally because there are separate competition classes for cars, trucks, motorbikes and quadbikes. The 2010 Rally featured 57 cars, 28 trucks, 88 motorbikes and 14 quadbikes. In 1992, Ethiopia's Hubert Auriol became the first person to win the Dakar both in a car (1992) and on a motorbike (1981).

Strenuous stages

The rally is split up into a series of stages; mostly over distances of between 200–600km (125–370 miles). The racing is a real test of endurance over many days, not only for the drivers but also the vehicles, which have to deal with all sorts of conditions from rocky plains to mud and sand dunes.

Dakar legends

In 2001, Germany's Jutta Kleinschmidt became the first woman to win the Dakar Rally. Six years later, France's Stéphane Peterhansel won his third Dakar Rally in a car. This was in addition to his astonishing six wins in the motorcycle class.

German driver Jutta Kleinschmidt and her co-driver Fabrizio Pons, from Italy, **navigate** the desert dunes during the first stage of the Dakar Rally.

GREAT SPORTING STATS

In the Dakar Rally, trucks are classed as vehicles weighing more than 3,500kg. The Kamaz racing team from Russia has the best record in the truck racing category of the Dakar Rally, having won nine rallies in total.

Formula 1

Formula 1 (F1) cars are highly advanced, open-wheel racing cars that cost tens of millions of pounds to develop. They feature in a worldwide championship of Grand Prix races – the most popular motorsports competition in the world.

Cream of the crop

Racing drivers all over the world start out with the dream of racing in Formula 1. There are many levels of racing below F1, with GP2 considered to be the competition just one step below Formula 1. Success in that competition can lead to being offered a place in a Formula 1 team. British driver Lewis Hamilton, for example, became GP2 champion in 2006 and moved up to F1 the following year.

Around the world

In the first Formula 1 season in 1950, there were just seven races. Recent seasons have featured 18 or 19 races, with the season beginning in March and ending in November. In between, F1 teams travel to Australia, Japan, Canada, China and many other countries. Teams develop and refine their technology throughout a race season and drivers often have to adapt to new versions of their cars.

Lorenzo Bandini of Italy races in his Ferrari Formula 1 car at the 1966 United States Grand Prix.

Britain's Lewis Hamilton makes a pit stop in his McLaren Mercedes car during the 2009 Chinese Grand Prix. Pit teams can refuel a car in under six seconds.

Grand Prix races

The week of a Formula 1 race begins with practice sessions and then qualifying, usually the day before the race, to determine each car's position on the **starting grid**. Races are around 305km (190 miles) long and are completed in around 90 minutes of intense racing. Cars can accelerate from a standstill to 160km/h (100mph) in just 3.5 seconds, and can reach top speeds of 340km/h (211mph).

Rule changes

Changes to the racing rules occur frequently in Formula 1. In the 2010 season, for example, refuelling during races was banned. This led to fuel tanks enlarging to around three times their former capacity.

GREAT SPORTING STATS

In 2010, a new points system for Formula 1 was introduced, with cars finishing from first to tenth place gaining points. Here are the new points for places with the previous points system in brackets.

1st 25 (10)
2nd 18 (8)
3rd 15 (6)
4th 12 (5)
5th 10 (4)
6th 8 (3)
7th 6 (2)
8th 4 (1)
9th 2 (0)
10th 1 (0)

Famous F1 races and drivers

Points in each F1 race count towards two separate competitions – the Drivers' Championship for individual racers and the Constructors' Championship for the race teams they drive for. In 2010, Sebastian Vettel won the drivers' crown and his team Red Bull the constructors' title.

Sebastian Vettel of Germany raises the trophy for winning the 2010 Abu Dhabi Grand Prix and, as a result, the World Championship.

Championship winners

Ferrari has been the most successful team in Formula 1, having taken part since it began in 1950, and winning over 210 races and 16 Constructors' Championships. Germany's Michael Schumacher with an astonishing 91 Formula 1 race wins and seven Drivers' Championships is the most successful F1 driver of all time.

Different circuits

Part of Formula 1's appeal is how the race circuits differ greatly from one another. Some, such as Monaco and the Singapore Grand Prix tracks, run through city streets. Others are on permanent dedicated race circuits, such as Hockenheim in Germany and Monza in Italy.

The Monaco Grand Prix circuit is a thrilling ride, with many twists and hairpin bends.

The Monaco Grand Prix

First held in 1929, the Monaco Grand Prix is one of the highlights of Formula 1's year. The race is held on Monaco's public roads, which are converted every year into a twisting, turning 3.34km (2 mile) circuit. It is one of the toughest tests of a driver's skills, with hundreds of sharp changes in speed and tight bends requiring over 4,000 gear changes during the 78-lap race.

Germany's Sebastian Vettel was 21 years and 73 days old when he won the Italian Grand Prix in 2008 and became the youngest ever race winner. Two years later, he won the Formula 1 World Championship, again the youngest ever driver to do so.

Triple crown

The Monaco Grand Prix, along with the Indianapolis 500 and the Le Mans 24 Hours race, are known as motorsports' triple crown. Only one man has won all three events – Britain's Graham Hill, in the 1960s and 70s.

Motocross championships

Motocross is an exciting motorcycle sport that begins when up to 40 riders gather for a massed start. They race a number of laps of a closed off-road style circuit, complete with dips, bumps, hills and jumps. The aim is to cross the finish line first to gain maximum points.

Tough racing

Top level motocross races last around 30–40 minutes and place enormous strains on a rider's strength and reactions. Close racing and the obstacles on the course often take their toll and crashes and falls are common. Riders are protected with a full-face helmet and padded racing leathers.

Motocross bikes

Motocross bikes are light but sturdily built, with long saddles for riders to shift their weight around as they jump, land and throw their bikes into tight bends. Bikes race in different classes based on their engine sizes and capacities. The 125cc and 250cc classes are the most popular.

Grant Langston, of South Africa, leads the start of the AMA 125cc Motocross Championship. He went on to win.

24

AMA Motocross Championship

Motocross is run by a number of organisations. In the USA, the American Motorcyclist Association (**AMA**) is the leading body. Its championship is held between May and September over 12 different race days, each featuring two races with 25 points on offer for each race win. In 2010, the AMA 250cc competition attracted more than 100 riders throughout the season with the winner, Trey Canard, scoring 474 points.

The World Motocross Championship

In the rest of the world, the **FIM** (Fédération Internationale de Motocyclisme) runs a major motocross competition with 15 different race days, each with two races. Most circuits are in Europe, but occasionally races are held in North and South America. Since 2008, a Women's World Motocross Championship has been run over seven different European circuits. Germany's Stephanie Laier was champion in 2010.

GREAT SPORTING STATS

US rider Ricky Carmichael won seven AMA Motocross championships in a row (2000–2006). He was nicknamed the G.O.A.T., meaning Greatest Of All Time.

Motocross legend, Ricky Carmichael makes a flying jump on his bike during a Supercross series race in Florida, USA.

MotoGP

A motorcycling world championship was first held in 1949. In 2002 the 500cc motorbike class was renamed MotoGP with the introduction of 990cc engines. In 2007, 800cc bikes were introduced instead.

Monster motorbikes

MotoGP motorbikes are extremely powerful machines. They are built by major motorcycle manufacturers and are not available for sale to the public. No expense is spared in constructing these incredibly powerful bikes. In a practice round for the 2009 Italian Grand Prix, Spanish MotoGP rider Dani Pedrosa reached a record speed of 349.29km/h (217mph) on his Honda RC212V motorbike.

MotoGP season

A MotoGP season begins in April with the Qatar Grand Prix in the Middle East. The competition lasts 18 rounds and is held in 14–16 different countries, including Australia, Japan, Spain, Malaysia and the UK. Races vary in length, but usually take around 45 minutes, in which riders complete around 35 laps of a track.

Spain's Jorge Lorenzo leads a pack of MotoGP riders through a turn at the British Grand Prix at Donington circuit.

Italy's Valentino Rossi has an incredible record in motorcyle racing. In over 230 races, he has recorded 104 race wins. He has also finished in second or third place 69 times. Rossi has won the MotoGP world championship on six occasions (2002, 2003, 2004, 2005, 2008 and 2009).

Italy's Valentino Rossi reacts after winning the MotoGP race of the German Motorcycle Grand Prix, 2009.

Points winners

A MotoGP race winner receives 25 points, second place 20, third place 16, fourth place 13, down to fifteenth place with one point. Over a season, a top rider strives to not only win races but also to make sure that they gain points in the races they don't win. In 2009, Italian racer Valentino Rossi won six races but also finished second, third or fourth an impressive eight times to win his sixth MotoGP World Championship.

Timeline and winner tables

1894 The first organised motor race occurs; a city-to-city race between Paris and Rouen.

1906 The first major Italian road race, the Targa Florio, is run.

1911 The first Indy 500 race.

1923 The first running of the 24 Hours of Le Mans.

1927 Opening of the legendary Nordschleife track at the Nürburgring in Germany.

1929 The first Monaco Grand Prix.

1950 The first Formula 1 Grand Prix championship season.

1950 NASCAR's first 500-mile race, the Southern 500, is held.

1957 Argentina's Juan Manuel Fangio becomes the oldest ever F1 world champion at the age of 47.

1958 US driver Richard Petty enters NASCAR for the first time. He goes on to win 200 races.

1959 The Daytona International Speedway is opened.

1966 Italy's Giacomo Agostini wins the first of eight Grand Prix motorcycling world championships.

1972 The first stadium motocross event held in Los Angeles, USA.

1972 Britain's Graham Hill becomes the first to win the Indy 500, the Formula 1 World Championship and the Le Mans 24 Hours.

1973 The World Rally Championship begins.

1975 Italy's Lella Lombardi becomes the first female driver to win Formula 1 championship points, coming sixth in the Spanish Grand Prix.

1978 The first running of the Paris-Dakar Rally, later known as the Dakar Rally.

1981 France's Michele Mouton becomes the first woman to win a World Rally Championship event, the Sanremo rally.

1987 The Suzuka circuit in Japan becomes a Formula 1 race for the first time.

1999 Finland's Tommi Mäkinen becomes the first driver to win the World Rally Championship four times in a row.

2001 Germany's Jutta Kleinschmidt becomes the first woman to win the Dakar Rally.

2002 The MotoGP competition begins, replacing the 500cc Grand Prix.

2008 Danica Patrick, of the USA, becomes the first woman to win an IndyCar race.

2010 Germany's Sebastian Vettel wins his first Formula 1 World Championship.

2010 Jimmie Johnson becomes the first NASCAR driver to win five championships in a row.

Formula 1 cars race in the 1960s.

Winner tables

Formula 1 Championship

Year	Driver	Team
2010	Sebastian Vettel (Germany)	Red Bull (Austria)
2009	Jenson Button (Britain)	Brawn (Britain)
2008	Lewis Hamilton (Britain)	McLaren (Britain)
2007	Kimi Räikkönen (Finland)	Ferrari (Italy)
2006	Fernando Alonso (Spain)	Renault (France)
2005	Fernando Alonso (Spain)	Renault (France)
2004	Michael Schumacher (Germany)	Ferrari (Italy)
2003	Michael Schumacher (Germany)	Ferrari (Italy)

NASCAR Nextel/Sprint Cup

Year	Driver	Vehicle make
2010	Jimmie Johnson	Chevrolet
2009	Jimmie Johnson	Chevrolet
2008	Jimmie Johnson	Chevrolet
2007	Jimmie Johnson	Chevrolet
2006	Jimmie Johnson	Chevrolet
2005	Tony Stewart	Chevrolet
2004	Kurt Busch	Ford
2003	Matt Kenseth	Ford
2002	Tony Stewart	Pontiac
2001	Jeff Gordon	Chevrolet
2000	Bobby Labonte	Pontiac

World Rally Championship

Year	Champion driver	Champion manufacturer
2010	Sébastien Loeb (France)	Citroën
2009	Sébastien Loeb (France)	Citroën
2008	Sébastien Loeb (France)	Citroën
2007	Sébastien Loeb (France)	Ford
2006	Sébastien Loeb (France)	Ford
2005	Sébastien Loeb (France)	Citroën
2004	Sébastien Loeb (France)	Citroën
2003	Petter Solberg (Norway)	Citroën
2002	Marcus Grönholm (Finland)	Peugeot
2001	Richard Burns (Britain)	Peugeot
2000	Marcus Grönholm (Finland)	Peugeot

MotoGP

Year	Champion rider	Champion vehicle
2010	Jorge Lorenzo (Spain)	Yamaha
2009	Valentino Rossi (Italy)	Yamaha YZR-M1
2008	Valentino Rossi (Italy)	Yamaha YZR-M1
2007	Casey Stoner (Australia)	Ducati Desmosedici GP07
2006	Nicky Hayden (USA)	Honda RC211V
2005	Valentino Rossi (Italy)	Yamaha YZR-M1
2004	Valentino Rossi (Italy)	Yamaha YZR-M1
2003	Valentino Rossi (Italy)	Honda RC211V
2002	Valentino Rossi (Italy)	Honda RC211V
2001	Valentino Rossi (Italy)	Honda NSR500
2000	Kenny Roberts Jr. (USA)	Suzuki RGV500

Glossary and further info

Accelerate To increase speed.

AMA Short for the American Motorcyclist Association, the body which organises and promotes the leading motorcycle racing competitions in the USA.

Amateur A driver, rider or team not paid to take part in motorsports competitions.

Asphalt A sticky oil-based substance, used to provide a smooth and hardwearing top surface on tracks and roads.

Circuit Another name for tracks used in car and motorcycle racing events.

Cockpit The space in a car for the driver.

Co-driver The name given to the navigator in a rally car, who gives the driver course instructions as they race.

Endurance To be able to do something for a long period of time.

Ethanol A type of fuel made from alcohol.

Field The number of vehicles in a motor race.

FIM Short for *Fédération Internationale de Motocyclisme*, the body which runs many leading world motorcycling competitions.

Handling How a car responds when racing, changing speeds and altering direction.

Navigate In rallying, to plot a route from one place to another.

Open-wheel Types of racing cars, usually single-seater vehicles, with their wheels outside of their bodies.

Photo finish When two or more competitors in a race cross the finishing line at the same time, a photo is used to tell who the winner is.

Pit stop When a car or bike leaves the racetrack and enters a pit area to receive fuel, tyre changes or repairs.

Pole sitter (also known as pole position) The driver with the best position at the front of a starting grid, because his car or bike has qualified with the fastest time.

Qualifying Races or timed sessions that decide the order of the starting grid at the beginning of a race.

Rolling start When race vehicles perform preliminary laps of the track and are on the move as the race starts.

Starting grid The area of the track where cars line up just before a race starts.

Stock car A form of motor racing on tracks using modified versions of cars produced for sale to the public.

Suspension The system of springs, shock absorbers and other parts which are joined to the wheels or axles and affect how a car or bike handles.

Websites

http://www.autoracing1.com
An American motorsports website with news on major competitions including NASCAR, Formula 1 and IndyCar racing.

http://www.crash.net
This website carries in-depth news and details of Formula 1 and MotoGP racing, as well as other classes of motorsport.

http://www.motorsport.com
This comprehensive website features competition news, race dates and the results of major events from the Dakar Rally to Indycars.

http://www.fia.com
The official website of the Fédération Internationale de l'Automobile.

http://www.fim-live.com/en
The FIM runs many of the world's major motorcycling racing competitions including Enduro and MotoGP.

http://www.formula1.com
Formula 1's official website is full of in-depth features on the drivers, teams, the technology and guides to the race circuits.

http://www.nascar.com
The official NASCAR racing website has pages filled with information on teams, drivers, races and technology.

http://www.wrc.com/index.jsp
The official website of the World Rally Championships, with a complete schedule of the current season, driver profiles, photos and video footage.

http://www.motogp.com
The official MotoGP website includes news, exciting photos and videos of race action.

http://www.ama-cycle.org
The home of the American Motorcyclist Association (AMA)'s racing division, including links to motocross and other competitions.

http://www.planetlemans.com
This website focuses on the Le Mans 24 Hours competition as well as other forms of endurance racing.

http://www.dakar.com
The official website of the Dakar Rally is packed with profiles of leading drivers and detailed course maps.

http://www.indycar.com
The official website of the IndyCar Series has full details of races, results and video clips.

http://www.rallye-info.com/Default.asp
Use this website to keep up-to-date with all the latest news in rally racing.

Further reading

The Kingfisher Motorsports Encyclopedia – Clive Gifford (Kingfisher, 2006)
A detailed guide to all forms of motorsport.

Go Turbo: Formula 1 – Tom Palmer (Franklin Watts, 2009)
Find out more about Formula 1, from top drivers to the best circuits.

Index